# Mobile Testing

Frequently asked Interview Q & A

(Android & iOS Testing)

By *Bandana Ojha*

# Introduction

This book contains most frequently asked mobile testing interview questions and answers. It will help the reader to get a good understanding of android & iOS testing, methodology, concept, approaches and design patterns. This book is aimed at anyone who is interested to take a job in mobile testing ranging from junior to expert level. The authors of this book conducted so many interviews at various companies and meticulously collected the most effective questions with simple, straightforward explanations. Rather than going through comprehensive, textbook-sized reference guides, this book includes only the information required immediately for mobile testing interview to start their career in software industry. Answers of all the questions are short and to the point. We assure that you will get here the 90% frequently asked interview questions and answers.

*Good luck to all who is preparing for android and iOS testing.*

Please check this out:

Our other best-selling books

500+ Java & J2EE Interview Questions & Answers-Java & J2EE Programming

200+ Frequently Asked Interview Questions & Answers in iOS Development

200 + Frequently Asked Interview Q & A in SQL , PL/SQL, Database Development & Administration

100+ Frequently Asked Interview Questions & Answers in Scala

100+ Frequently Asked Interview Q & A in Swift Programming

100+ Frequently Asked Interview Q & A in Python Programming

100+ Frequently Asked Interview Questions & Answers in Android Development

100+ most Frequently Asked Interview Questions & Answers in Manual Testing

Frequently asked Interview Q & A in Java programming

Frequently Asked Interview Questions & Answers in J2EE

Frequently asked Interview Q & A in Mobile Testing

Frequently asked Interview Q & A in Test Automation-Selenium Testing

# 1. What are different testing frameworks?

Framework is basically a testing automation framework used as an execution environment to perform automated tests. It is defined as a set of assumptions, concepts, and practices which establish a work platform or support for automated testing.

A testing framework is responsible for

-Defining a format to express expectations

-Creating a mechanism to hook into or drive the application under test

-Executing the tests and reporting the results

# 2. What is the Android testing strategy?

The standard Android testing strategy must include the following test

Unit Test

Integration Test

Operation Test

System Test

# 3. List out the best practices for Android Testing?

Developer should prepare the test cases at the same time when they are writing the code

Together with source code all test cases should be stored

Use continuous integration and execute tests every time the code is changed

Avoid using rooted devices and emulators

# 4.Can mobile application testing be automated?

Yes, it can be. The fact that mobile application testing is gradually grasping the attention of IT industry may be the reason why several mobile test automation tools like TestingWhiz, TestComplete, M-Eux, Robotium etc. for mobile app testing are being released into the market. It is best to keep your options open and explore all forms of mobile application testing and choose the ones that best suit your needs.

## 5.What is the difference between Mobile testing and mobile application testing?

Mobile testing (MT) means testing the mobile device and mobile application testing

(MAT) means testing of the mobile application on a mobile device.

MAT focuses on features and functionality of a tested application while MT focus on native features like Media player, buttons, SMS, Call, etc.

## 6. What is the difference between Web testing and WAP testing?

Web Testing: It is related mainly to the testing of web applications such as websites and portals

WAP Testing: It is the testing of WAP (Wireless Application Protocol) used in network applications

## 7. What are the types of mobile app testing?

The types of mobile app testing include

Usability Testing

Compatibility Testing

Interface testing

Services testing

Performance Testing

Operational testing

Installation tests

Security Testing

## 8. What are the types of mobile applications?

Mobile applications are of three types:

Native Application– Native app installed from application store like Android's google play store and apple' app store. A Native App is an app developed essentially for one mobile device and is installed directly onto the device itself. The native app can work much faster by harnessing the power of the processor. and can access specific hardware like GPS, accelerometer, compass, list of contacts, and so on. One example of native app is WhatsApp.

Web Application– Web apps are basically websites with interactivity that feels like a mobile app. Web app runs from mobile web browsers like Chrome, Firefox, Opera, Safari etc.and are written in HTML5 and/or JavaScript. The downside is that web apps can be slower, less intuitive, and inaccessible through app stores. Examples of Web apps are m.facebook.com, m.gmail.com, m.yahoo.com, etc.

Hybrid Application- A hybrid app combines elements of both native and web apps. Hybrid apps can be distributed through the app stores just like a native app, and they can incorporate operating system features. Like a web app, hybrid apps also use cross-compatible web technologies. Hybrid apps are typically easier and faster to develop and require less maintenance. On the other hand, the speed of your hybrid app will depend completely on the speed of the internet to which user is connected. Examples, eBay, amazon etc.

## 9. What is the basic difference between Emulator and Simulator?

Emulator mimics the mobile device software, hardware and operating system.

Simulator mimics the internal behavior of the device.

Emulator is written in machine-level assembly language. Simulator is written

in high-level language.

Emulator is more suitable for debugging.

Simulator is faster than emulators.

## 10. What are the common challenges in mobile application testing?

Working on different operating systems, a variety of handsets, different networks, a variety of screen sizes etc.

## 11. What is the strategy used to test new mobile app?

System integration testing

Functional testing

Installation and uninstallation of the app

Test HTML control

Performance

Check in multiple mobile OS

Cross browser and cross-device testing

Gateway testing

Network and Battery testing

## 12. When to choose automation testing and when manual testing?

Manual Testing

If the application has new functionality

If the application requires testing once or twice

Automate Testing

If the regression tests are repeated

Testing app for complex scenarios

## 13. What are the tools based on cloud based mobile testing?

Seetest

Perfecto Mobile

BlazeMeter

AppThwack

Manymo

DeviceAnywhere etc.

## 14. Name mobile automation testing tools you know?

Ranorex

EggPlant

SOASTA

Appium

Robotium

KeepItFunctional(KIT)

Calabash

## 15.Can we use QTP/UFT for mobile automation testing?

Yes, with the help of Seetest add-in.

## 16. What are the defects tracking tools used for mobile testing?

You can use same testing tool which you use for web application testing like QC, Jira, Rally, Bugzilla etc.

## 17. What all major networks to be considered while performing application testing?

You should test the application on 5G, 4G, 3G, 2G, and WIFI. 2G is a slower network, it's good if you verify your application on a slower network also to track your application performance.

## 18. What does a test plan for Mobile App contain?

Test plan for mobile app is very similar to software app

Objective

Automation tools required

features to be tested

features not to be tested

Test cases

Test Strategy

Tested by

Time required

No. of resources required

## 19. List out the features do monkey tool provides?

Monkey tool provides features like

Basic configuration options

Operational constraints

Event types and frequencies

Debugging options

## 20. What is port testing?

This testing is done to test the same functionality on different devices with different platforms. It is classified into two categories
Device Testing
Platform Testing

## 21.What web services are used by mobile app?

They are many depend upon the application. SOAP and REST web services are used but RESTful is more common now.

## 22.What all devices have you worked till now?

Android, Windows, iPhone, Symbian etc.

## 23. While performing end to end mobile testing what are the major criteria, you must take in consideration?

Installation and uninstallation of the application

Verify the device in different available networks like 2G, 3G, 4G, 5G or WIFI.

Functional testing

Interrupt testing- Able to receive the calls while running the application.

Compatibility testing – Able to attach the photo in message from gallery

Test application performance on different handset.

Make some negative testing by entering the invalid credentials and test the behavior of the application

## 24. List out the most common problem that tester faces while doing mobile testing in Cloud Computing?

Challenges that tester faces while doing mobile testing are

Subscription model

High Costing

Lock-in

Internet connectivity issues

Automation is image based and time-consuming

Automation cannot be used outside the framework

## 25. What does mobile security testing include?

Mobile security testing includes

Checks for multi-user support without interfering with the data between them

Checks for access to files stored in the app by any unintended users

Decryption or Encryption method used for sensitive data communication

Detect sensitive areas in tested application so that they do not receive any malicious content

## 26. What is the latest version of iOS?

iOS 11 is the latest version of iOS. (changes often please check before you going to appear the interview)

## 27. What is the latest version of Android?

Oreo 8.1 is the latest version of Android. (changes quite often please check

before you going to appear the interview)

## 28. What is the latest version of Windows?

Windows 10 is the latest version of Windows. (changes quite often please check

before you going to appear the interview)

## 29. What is the extension of Android files?

. apk (Android application package)

## 30. What is the extension of iOS files?

. ipa is the extension of iOS files.

## 31. How to test CPU usage on mobile devices?

There are various tools available in the market like google play or app store from where you can install apps like CPU Monitor, Usemon, CPU Stats, CPU-Z etc. these are an advanced tool which records historical information about processes running on your device

## 32. What is the difference between an app and a widget?

A mobile app is a computer program designed to run on smartphones, tablets and other internet-connected devices. They are most commonly available through distribution services such as Google Play and Apple's App Store and can be free or paid. An app can be aimed at productivity, functionality or entertainment, and the term "app" represents the full functionality of a program from its main content to any peripheral features such as search, posting and activation. Opening an app results in a new screen in most cases, temporarily changing the primary function of the smartphone to the primary function of the app.

Widgets are another type of mobile computer program, and their main purpose is to make apps easier to use as well as enable multitasking. Widgets are extensions of apps, and give users access to the most frequently used functions of an app to reduce the need to open the full program. Widgets are almost always free, but usually cannot be used without the main app.

## 33. What do you mean by Streaming media?

Ans. Streaming is a process of downloading the data from the server. Streaming media is

the multimedia that is transferred from server or provider to the receiver.

## 34. List out some iPhone and iPad testing tools?

iPhone tester: Test your web interface in an iPhone sized frame

Appium: It is a test automation tool used with native and hybrid iOS application

iPad Peek: Test your web application using an iPad interface

Test Studio: It enables you to record, build and run automated tests for your iPad and iPhone applications.

## 35. What are the different types of mobile application testing?

Functional Testing

User Interface Testing

Usability Testing

Performance Testing

Stress Testing

Compatibility Testing

Interruption Testing

## 36. What are the best ways to carry out mobile application testing?

Mobile application testing is not just about writing test cases and executing them. Below are some pointers that can help a tester test mobile application in the most effective manner.

Explore and learn about mobile phones and their attributes. Domain knowledge will really help you see beyond the obvious.

Understand when, how and where the application will be used and then create test cases.

Study the mobile phones on which the applications will run and write appropriate test cases.

Use simulators as often as possible to execute the test cases.

Use remote device services (RDA) as well.

## 37.Name debugging tools for mobile?

Errors can be verified by the generated logs. We can use configuration utility on iOS and android monitor.bat on android. Here are few to name Android DDMS, Remote Debugging on Android with Chrome, Debugging from Eclipse with ADT, Android Debug Bridge, iOS simulator etc.

## 38. Explain what is Robo-electric testing framework?

Testing done on Android Testing Framework for emulators or device is difficult. Running and building test case sometimes takes lots of development effort. Robo-electric framework allows you to run Android test directly on JVM without the need of a device or an emulator.

## 39. While performing end to end mobile testing what are the major criteria, you must take in consideration?

Installation

Application launching without having network

Uninstallation of app

Orientation of app if it supports

Testing application performance on a different kind of devices and network scenarios

Testing the application response how it is responding

## 40. What are some tools used to capture app logs on Android?

We can use monitor.bat file located under tools folder of android sdk to see log and we can select and save the log from it. other than this alogcat is a free log getting tool which is present in Google Play

## 41. Tell about filter, how you can create while checking logs?

Filters helps you in finding relevant information about your application and you can create filter based on the application package name like com.abc.com and save this filter by name as My application, when you click on this filter then you will see only logs which are from your application. You can create filter based on Log tag which is related to the thing that line is doing example if you have placed system. Out to print the output put then you can create a filter by tag System. Out, then it will short list all the print output.

And you can create filter by Choreographer which helps in finding the skipped frames if you want to see it.

You can create filter corresponding to your PID and log message which is coming as text also.

## 42. Explain how A/B testing is done for iOS app?

A/B testing for iOS includes three steps

Configure a test: It prepares two versions of your iOS app (A&B) and test metric

Test: Tests two iOS versions above on devices simultaneously

Analyze: It select and measure better version to release

## 43. What are the modes of downloading content on mobile, from server?

There are many techniques to download a content e.g. downloading, progressive downloading, streaming etc.

Downloading: Normal download and can be saved in the local machine, once saved user can play or do operation whatever he likes.

Progressing downloading: Whenever user selects a content it starts buffering and the same will be continued till the file ends playing. The content will be played once the buffer is finished. This could be even a min (e.g. if the buffer is completed for 1 sec the content will be played for one second)

Streaming: When user selects a content to download, buffering takes place and once the buffer is over content will be played. Until then player does not get initiated. And user can save, play again or whatever the operation he requires.

## 44. What are Intents?

Intents displays notification messages to the user from within the Android enabled device. It can be used to alert the user of a state that occurred. Users can be made to respond to intents.

## 45. What is adb?

Android Debug Bridge (adb) is a versatile command-line tool that lets you communicate with a device. The adb command facilitates a variety of device actions, such as installing and debugging apps, and it provides access to a Unix shell that you can use to run a variety of commands on a device. It is a client-server program that includes three components:

A client, which sends commands. The client runs on your development machine. You can invoke a client from a command-line terminal by issuing an adb command.

A daemon (adbd), which runs commands on a device. The daemon runs as a background process on each device.

A server, which manages communication between the client and the daemon. The server runs as a background process on your development machine.

## 46. What is Android?

It is an open-sourced operating system that is used primarily on mobile devices, such as cell phones and tablets. It is a Linux kernel-based system that's been equipped with rich components that allows developers to create and run apps that can perform both basic and advanced functions.

## 47. How do you remove icons and widgets from the main screen of the Android device?

To remove an icon or shortcut, press and hold that icon. You then drag it downwards to the lower part of the screen where a remove button appears.

## 48. What language is supported by Android for application development?

The main language supported is Java programming language. Java is the most popular language for app development, which makes it ideal even for new Android developers to quickly learn to create and deploy applications in the Android environment.

## 49. What tools you use for performance testing and automation?

For Performance testing of the Web service which your application uses you can use jMeter, it is an open source tool which can be used to test the api's performances.
For Automation: It is very subjective term & totally depends on the project need and type of application , there are several paid tools available in the market like SeeTest, Ranorex, Silk Mobile etc. while good free automation tools are  Calabash, Appium , Robotium for Android, KIF for iOS and using free tools you require some coding skills like ruby or Java.

## 50. One thing which you cannot do with Emulator but can do with real device?

You can test the interrupts like phone call, messages, battery drain out completely while you were using the application under test, low battery scenarios etc.  on real devices, memory card mount/unmount scenarios, actual performance of your application can be test on real devices only, Bluetooth related testing can be only done on real devices.

## 51.When does ANR occur?

The ANR dialog is displayed to the user, based on two possible conditions. One is when there is no response to an input event within 5 seconds, and the other is when a broadcast receiver is not done executing within 10 seconds.

## 52. List out the most common problem that tester faces while doing mobile testing in Cloud Computing?

Challenges that tester faces while doing mobile testing are

Subscription model

High Costing

Lock-in

Internet connectivity issues

Automation is image based and time-consuming

Automation cannot be used outside the framework

## 53. Which activity in the fundamental test process includes evaluation of the testability of the requirements and system?

A 'Test Analysis' and 'Design' includes evaluation of the testability of the requirements and system.

## 54. What is negative and positive testing?

A negative test is when you put in an invalid input and receives errors. While a positive testing, is when you put in a valid input and expect some action to be completed in accordance with the specification.

## 55. What is Fault Masking?

Error condition hiding another error condition.

## 56. How you can eliminate the product risk in your project?

To eliminate product risk in your project, there is simple yet crucial step that can reduce the product risk in your project.

Investigate the specification documents

Have discussions about the project with all stakeholders including the developer

As a real user walk around the website

## 57. What is Fuzz testing and when it is used?

Fuzz testing is used to detect security loopholes and coding errors in software. In this technique random data is added to the system in attempt to crash the system. If vulnerability persists, a tool called fuzz tester is used to determine potential causes. This technique is more useful for bigger projects but only detects major fault.

## 58. Mention what are the basic components of defect report format?

The basic components of defect report format include

Project Name

Module Name

Defect detected on

Defect detected by

Defect ID and Name

Snapshot of the defect

Priority and Severity status

Defect resolved by

Defect resolved on

## 59. While testing iOS application on device, what you need to consider?

application functionality – functional testing

configuration settings – in settings section

impact of other application/hardware on application under test – like battery life, other application running with high memory, sleep mode etc.

## 60. What's Code Coverage?

Code coverage is a metric that helps us to measure the value of our unit tests.

## 61. What is ABI?

ABIs are important when it comes to applications that use external libraries. If a program is built to use a library and that library is later updated, you don't want to have to re-compile that application (and from the end-user's standpoint, you may not have the source). If the updated library uses the same ABI, then your program will not need to change.

## 62. Why is design pattern very important?

Design patterns are reusable solutions to common problems in software design. They're templates designed to help you write code that's easy to understand and reuse. Most common Cocoa design patterns:

Creational: Singleton.

Structural: Decorator, Adapter, Facade.

Behavioral: Observer, and, Memento

## 63. Explain what is defer?

Defer keyword which provides a block of code that will be executed in the case when execution is leaving the current scope.

## 64. What is KVC—KVO?

KVC stands for Key-Value Coding. It's a mechanism by which an object's properties can be accessed using strings at runtime rather than having to statically know the property names at development time.

KVO stands for Key-Value Observing and allows a controller or class to observe changes to a property value. In KVO, an object can ask to be notified of any changes to a specific property, whenever that property changes value, the observer is automatically notified.

## 65. What is Operator Overloading?

Operator overloading allows us to change how existing operators behave with types that both already exist.

## 66. What is Dynamic Dispatch?

Dynamic Dispatch is the process of selecting which implementation of a polymorphic operation that's a method or a function to call at run time. This means, that when we want to invoke our methods like object method. but Swift does not default to dynamic dispatch.

## 67. What is the difference between Synchronous & Asynchronous task?

Synchronous: waits until the task has completed

Asynchronous: completes a task in background and can notify you when complete

## 68. Mention what should be the selecting criteria for Test Automation Tool for mobile Testing?

For mobile testing, the test automation tool should have following criteria

Multi-platform support: Ensure that the tool does support your current and future target platform

Script Usability: Object-based tools provides a high degree of the script usability

Jailbreak Requirement: If the tool uses rooted devices, it may not support latest OS version and may be incompatible with MDM policies

Source Code Changes: Sharing source code may not be possible always

Lead time for New OS version: How soon tool can support new iOS/android/iOS/android/another OS version

## 69. What do you understand by comparison testing?

This is a question that looks difficult but is framed in such a manner. Comparison is nothing but comparing your application with that of your competitor. All that you would do during comparison testing is to compare the app you have developed with that of your competitors'. You could compare the speed, quality, user interface, quality and other parameters as decided by you or your client.

## 70. What is the difference between User Agent and Simulator?

User Agent is mandatory while downloading appropriate contents onto mobile, whereas a
simulator is used to test the downloading process using various user agents to check whether a device is recognized, and specific content/build is sent through OTA.

## 71. What is GPRS?

General Packet Radio Services (GPRS) is a non-voice wireless Internet technology that is very popular since it can support both phone calls and Internet data transmission. Some GSM, or Global System for Mobile Communications, mobile phones can even handle both phone communication and Internet access at the same time. It transmits data packets on GSM systems where cell phone channels are shared.

## 72. How GPRS Works?

In GSM cell phone systems, there will always be idle radio capacity. This is the capacity of a network provider that is not being used and it stays unused until other cell phone users decide to make phone calls. GPRS uses this idle radio capacity to establish a data network to be used for data transmission. If a network provider's idle radio capacity decreases, which means a lot of phone calls are being serviced, data transmission and speed decreases as well. Cell phone calls have a higher priority than Internet data transmission in cell phone network providers.

## 73. How GPRS is different from GPS?

GPS and GPRS are far different when it comes to functionality even though there's only one letter that differ. As a technology, GPS stands for Global Positioning System which can track different sites on Earth as it receives data from satellites, while GPRS connects with the cell sites for signals to provide service for cellular phones.

## 74. What are the different classes of GPRs? What is the use of this GPRs classes?

There are three classes:

Class A

Class B

Class c

Class A : Can be connected to GPRS service and GSM service (voice, SMS), using both at the same time. Such devices are known to be available today.

Class B : Can be connected to GPRS service and GSM service (voice, SMS), but using only one or the other at a given time. During GSM service (voice call or SMS), GPRS service is suspended, and then resumed automatically after the GSM service (voice call or SMS) has concluded. Most GPRS mobile devices are Class B.

Class C :  Are connected to either GPRS service or GSM service (voice, SMS). Must be switched manually between one or the other service.

## 75. What kind of testing do you perform (functional, interruption, connectivity, etc.)?

Very first test we must perform installation, after that we check the basic functionality and after that we check the connectivity related stuff of the application, then we uninstall the build and verify how application respond when we interrupt during installation and, we check interruption scenarios when our application request network call.

We also do low network/poor connectivity testing during network call. Upgrade from older version to newer version. navigation in the application without network if it supports this feature. Compatibility of app on different kind of phones like having external buttons & devices do not have external buttons or other than this flip phone etc.

## 76. What is An Intent?

It is connected to either the external world of application or internal world of application, such as, opening a pdf is an intent and connect to the web browser.

## 77. What is sleep mode in android?

Sleep mode mean CPU will be sleeping, and it doesn't accept any commands from android device except Radio interface layer and alarm.

## 78. What is Coverage status, what does it do?

Coverage status is percentage of testing covered at a given time and to keep track of project deadline.

## 79. Why is the use of a filter?

Filter is used to view the data based on user criteria and Filters are available for Graphs, Reports and Grids.

## 80. What is container in android?

The container holds objects, widgets, labels, fields, icons, buttons'.

## 81. What are some common execution states in iOS?

The common execution states are as follows:

Not Running: The app is completely switched off; no code is being executed.

Inactive: The app is running in the foreground without receiving any events.

Active: The app is running in the foreground and receiving events.

Background: The app is executing code in the background.

Suspended: The app is in the background but is not executing any code.

## 82. Name four important data types found in Objective-C.

Four important data types found in Objective -C are

NSString: Represents a string.

CGfloat: Represents a floating-point value.

NSInteger: Represents an integer.

BOOL: Represents a Boolean.

## 83.What is made up of NSError object?

There are three parts of NSError object a domain, an error code, and a user info dictionary. The domain is a string that identifies what categories of errors this error is coming from.

## 84. Is cloud base mobile testing possible? Name any?

Yes, cloud based mobile testing possible.

Perfecto Mobile and Seetest.

## 85. What's the difference between the frame and the bounds?

The bounds of an UIView is the rectangle, expressed as a location (x, y) and size (width, height) relative to its own coordinate system (0,0).

The frame of an UIView is the rectangle, expressed as a location (x, y) and size (width, height) relative to the super view it is contained within.

## 86. Why is design pattern very important?

Design patterns are reusable solutions to common problems in software design. They're templates designed to help you write code that's easy to understand and reuse. Most common Cocoa design patterns:

Creational: Singleton.

Structural: Decorator, Adapter, Facade.

Behavioral: Observer, and, Memento

## 87. What are UI elements and some common ways you can add them to your app?

Buttons, text fields, images, labels, and any other elements that are visible within the application are called UI elements. These elements may be interactive and comprise the user interface (hence the term "UI") of an application. In iOS development, UI elements can be quickly added through Xcode's interface builder or coded from scratch and laid out using NSLayoutConstraints and Auto Layout. Alternatively, each element can also be positioned at exact coordinates using the UIView "(id)initWithFrame:(CGRect)frame" method.

## 88. Does Selenium support mobile internet testing?

Yes, it does, Opera browser is used for Mobile internet testing.

## 89. What is the difference between Synchronous & Asynchronous task?

Synchronous: waits until the task has completed

Asynchronous: completes a task in background and can notify you when complete

## 90. What is Operator Overloading?

Operator overloading allows us to change how existing operators behave with types that both already exist.

## 91. Grand Central Dispatch (GCD)?

GCD is a library that provides a low-level and object-based API to run tasks concurrently while managing threads behind the scenes.

## 92. How you can install SD card in emulator?

Create the mySdCardFile.img disk image:

mksdcard -l mySdCard 1024M mySdCardFile.img

Start two emulators with different AVDs. Use the -sdcard flag to specify the name and path of the disk image you created.

emulator -avd Pixel_API_25 -sdcard mySdCardFile.img

emulator -avd NEXUS_6_API_25 -sdcard mySdCardFile.img

## 93. What is MO Message?

Mo SMS Message means mobile originated SMS, i.e. the SMS is composed and sent from the Handset Under Test

## 94. What Is Benchmark Testing?

Benchmarking testing is the process of comparing application performance with respect to industry standard which is given by some other organization. Benchmark informs us where our application stands with respect to others. Benchmark compares our application performance with other company's application's performance.

## 95. What are different mobile testing platforms?

Before starting with mobile testing, it's better to understand the basics of mobile platforms. Basics include mobile operating system, type of the device, and type of the mobile app. Having enough knowledge on all these basics will help in performing strong test planning in the long run.

## 96. How to test a mobile application?

Mobile application testing is a process of testing an application software for its functionality, usability, and consistency. Mobile application testing can be done manually or can be automated.

## 97. Name different mobile application testing tools?

Below are different mobile application tools

Android

Android Lint

Find Bugs

iPhone

Clang Static Analyzer

Analyze code from XCode

## 98. What is robotium framework?

Robotium is an open-source test framework which is used for writing automatic grey-box test cases for Android applications. Using Robotium, test case developers can write function, system and acceptance test scenarios, spanning multiple Android activities.

Robotium can be used both for testing applications where the source code is available and applications where only the APK file is available.

## 99. Which things to consider testing a mobile application through black box technique?

By testing your application on multiple devices.

By changing the port and IP addresses to make sure the device is getting connected and     disconnected properly.

By making calls and sending messages to other devices.

By testing your web application on different mobile browsers like chrome, Firefox, opera, dolphin etc.

## 100. What is MT Message?

In general terms, if you send any SMS message and get SMS response for that message, then the sending message is called Message Originate(MO) and the response SMS message you receive is Message Terminate(MT).

## 101. Explain some test cases on mobile feature interaction testing?

There are so many mobile core applications Few TCs for feature interaction could be like

To able to receive calls while browsing in contacts.

To be able to attach photos in messages from gallery

To be able to receive calls while taking launching camera

To be able to receive Alarm notification in setting applications

Interview Q & A series -1
100+ frequently asked interview Q & A

**Manual**
TESTING

By Bandana Ojha

Interview Q&A Series-2

**Frequently asked Interview Q & A**

Test Automation

**Selenium Testing**
By Bandana Ojha

Interview Q & A Series -3

Frequently Asked

**Interview Q&A**
in Mobile Testing

iOS

By Bandana Ojha

Interview Q & A Series -4

Frequently asked

**Interview Q& A in Java**

Java

By Bandana Ojha

Interview Q & A Series-5

**FREQUENTLY ASKED INTERVIEW Q & A IN J2EE**

JSP — EJB
SERVLET — JMS
JDBC — JNDB

By Bandana Ojha

Interview Q & A Series-6

Frequently Asked

**500+ Java & J2EE Interview Q & A**

J2EE

Java

Java JSP Servlet EJB JMS JDBA JNDB
By Bandana Ojha

Interview Q&A Series- 7

Frequently Asked

**Interview Q & A**
in Python Programming

By Bandana Ojha